INWIT

For Paul,
with encouragement for
your own work.

Poems by LOLETTE KUBY

Lolette Kuby

Pearl's Book'em Publisher, Atlanta

On Lolette Kuby's Inwit:

"There lives the dearest freshness deep down things," said G.M. Hopkins. Lolette Kuby unerringly finds it - in a cherry blossom in March that has `gone out on a limb,` 'the reasons of grass,' a fox who 'rushes onto the pretty chickens causing breakfast/ and terror and knowledge.` There is 'nothing so patient as girders in dusky basements,/Bearing the whole house over them/Except in their seasonless dockage/ The dead;' a lion that lies upon the bloodiest breast of an antelope 'as though/ the two had completed an act of love,' and stares directly at the camera, 'unblinking/ and luminous. The face of a saint.'

Kuby brings the same honest and unblinking eye to all of her subjects - from love and sex to cockroaches. Poets of an earlier time used the term "Inwit" to describe a 'certaine and inward knowledge' that is instinctive in animals but in humans is the source of conscience (the 'agynbyte of Inwyt'), courage and the quickening of the soul. Caxton's Reynard speaks of 'Suche…so woo [miserable] lyke as they had loste theyr Inwytte.' Poems like 'Hi-Rise Haiku' and 'The Very Iris' remind us of the kind of knowledge we must hold on tight to.

On another level, Kuby's poems are about poetry itself -trying to stab, like a darting hummingbird, to the essence of a thing or moment or human interaction in such a way as to remind us of the real life 'goes on/outside these fragments.' The second part of Kuby's book, subtitled 'The Trade,' includes three drafts of an evolving poem and and illuminating afterthought about their relationship to the original inspiration; poignant meditations on the lives of Philip Larkin and Anne Sexton; confessions of a creative writing class enrolle; and a hilarious deconstruction of her own poem about the fox in the henhouse. Kuby's advice on how 'To Be a Poet' ('Come from a harsh father, and a mother/of whims… chase the light on the running ground') is worth the price of admission.

Dennis Dooley-Editor, "Northern Ohio Live"; Author of "Dashiell Hammett" and "Superman at Fifty: The Persistence of a Legend"; also the unpublished manuscripts "A Cloud in Trousers" (after Mayakovsky) and "The Essential Catullus."

Published by:
Pearl's Book'em Publisher
6300 Powers Ferry Rd
Suite 600, #272
Atlanta, GA 30339- USA

bookpearl@bookpearl.com

Printed and bound in the United States of America

Kuby, Lolette
Inwit

ISBN 0-9740520-2-7

Library of Congress Control Number: 2003094516

Kuby, Lolette.

Inwit : poems / by Lolette Kuby ; [edited by Pearlie
Harris, Shonia Brown]. -- Atlanta, Ga. : Pearl's
Book'em Publisher, 2003.

    p. ; cm.

    ISBN: 0-9740520-2-7 (pbk.)

    1. American poetry. I. Harris, Pearlie. II. Brown,
Shonia. III. Title.

PS3561.U22 A17 2003   2003094516
811/.6--dc22   0310

Acknowledgements

Ezra's Mother, Acts, *Northeast*; Second Love, *Event*; Craftsmen, *Hiram Review*; You Are, *Light Year '86* (anthol); For Philip Larkin, *American Scholar*; A Hitchcock Tale, *Prairie Schooner*; To a Lover, *Light Year '85* (anthol); War Story, The One Son, It Comes to This, *In Enormous Water* (chapbook); Immigrant Child, *Poet Lore*; The Lie, *Forum: Ten Poets of the Western Reserve*; My Soup, *The New Laurel Review*; Code, *Antigonish Review*; Just Watching, *The Long Story*; How To, *Whiskey Island*; Puzzle, *The Long Story*; Walking, *Canadian Woman Studies/cf*; The Trade, *The Denny Poems*; The Wrong Side of the Bed, *Midwest Quarterly*; Mmmm-Mmmm, *English Journal*; For Walt Whitman, *Mickle Street Review*; Forsythias, *The Heartlands Today* (anthol); Our Gift, *Canadian Woman Studies/cf..*

An Interview with Myself

You have been asked to say a few words about poetry and about your own poetry. What is poetry, anyway?
What is poetry, anyway? Poetry is language in which reality undergoes a sea-change. Reality is transformed.

But doesn't all literature do that—transform reality?
Yes. Probably all language does that. Okay. Poetry is a special heightened language. You know the quip about the Jewish People: They are like everyone else only more so. Well, poetry is like prose, only more so: more images, more metaphors, more symbols, more rhythm, all of which makes it more concentrated, denser—a richer soup than prose. And it is set up on the page in a funny way—a way that introduces two non-grammatical elements that have grammatical functions—the line end, and the caesura—ways of telling you to stop and breathe.

Wait a minute. I've read some pretty language-heightened novels and essays. You could set up Molly Bloom's "Yes" speech in *Ulysses*, for example, so it looks and sounds like poetry. The book *A Stone, A Leaf, A Door*, for another example, sets up passages from Thomas Wolfe's *You Can't Go Home Again*, so that anyone who didn't know would think it was written as poetry. Prose is full of that kind of possibility.
Well, that would be poetic prose. But I get your point. Okay. Poetry is the bursting through into language of love. Not just romantic love, of course, but love for a mother, a father, a child, a daffodil, a cloud, a dog, for the live oak growing in Louisiana. I'll bet everyone in the world has written a poem, and when? When they fall in love

Now, really. It's hard to think of a novel in which love doesn't "burst through." You'll have to do better than that.
But in the novel, it is always love in conflict, love in despair, love destroyed, love unrequited . . . In poems love is purified; it's there for its own sake, to celebrate that which is loved.

Oh? And how about,
   "Where have ye been, Lord Randall, my son?
   Where have ye been my handsome young one?
   I've been to my sweetheart, mother

. . .
And what did she give you, Lord Randall, my son?"

If you recall, his sweetheart gave him poison. You'll have to admit that there are as many poetic Desdemonas as prose Anna Kareninas. And don't drag out that old definition about prose having a plot—an end it travels toward—whereas poems present a kind of stasis. Because I am going to mention those ballads again, and poems like Frost's "The Generations of Men," or Browning's "Porphyria's Lover."
Okay. Poetry is different from prose in that it is always in some way, deep down, about death.

Nonsense! "In high Tibet there sits a Lama/got no papa, got no mama."
Poetry is the way a people record the stories of their origin, their values, their history. It is the vehicle of myth. Bards used to travel from village to village with these stories, which could be remembered more easily than prose because of rhyme and image and meter. After writing and other technologies replaced memory, poetry began to record personal myth. Yes. I'll stand on that. Poetry is the poet's record of his inner states, his private mythologies. If they could be deciphered, a poet's poems would give you a mythology of the poet's mind. Someone once said, "A poet is better known by his poems than his poems are by his life." Philip Larkin actually has a poem that touches that idea: "If my darling were once to decide . . . to jump. . . into my head/ She would find herself looped with the creep of varying light,/Monkey-brown, fish-grey, a string of infected circles . . ." Well, that's a glimpse Larkin's personal mythology. Think how different, say, Wordsworth's would be. Or maybe not.

But wouldn't you say memoirs and autobiographies are much more "personal mythologies" and require much less deciphering?
Well, I'm hard put. How about this: Poetry is an expression of the religious impulse. As with love, our deepest feelings of joy, our appeals to God, our thanks for life, our union with the universe wants to come out as poems. Look at *Psalms* and *The Song of Songs*, Hinduism's archaic Vedas, the Fourth Mundaka of the *Upanishads*. Look at Milton and Donne and Herbert and Merton and Rumi and . . .

Hold On! What are you going to do with Jesus or Meister Eckhart? And what are you going to do with poems that are intellectual games, like the ones that won a $40 thousand dollar prize a couple of years ago, that use only one kind of vowel in each poem; you have poems with only "e's and poems with only "u's, etc. How religious an impulse is that? You can argue with the taste of the judges, but poems containing only the letter "i" are poems nevertheless. Next you're going to tell me that a poem is something which, when it is destructured, leaves tracks that only a poem can leave.

No, I'm not going to tell you that, but I rather like it: "A poem is something which, when it is destructured, leaves tracks only a poem can leave."

Maybe we have to fall back on that non-definition that says that a poem is anything the poet thinks it is and anything a reader thinks it is—and they need not agree.

I'm not ready to concede to that. Okay, this is my final answer:

Poetry begins where prose leaves off. Prose is language that leads you to a worldview. Poetry is language that leads you into the silence.

And how about your poetry?

All of the above.

for Stephen

Contents

PART I   MIDNIGHT SNOW

DOCUMENTARY

The lion keeps eating, rips out
the belly of the antelope
and lies upon its breast as though
the two had completed an act
of love: one wet paw wears entrails
like a bright bracelet. The lion
licks its lips and stares directly
at the camera, unblinking
and luminous. The face of a saint.
The night is filled with passersby:
Children gnaw barbecued spareribs.
Lovers hold hands while their free hands
squeeze pizza into widened mouths.
A young mother offers her breast
to her bleating baby, now blissful.
Understand what I am getting at,
my friend? I see by your face you do.
Your lips are twitching.

ACTS

I act and he acts.
My act for him
Is that he be always
Arousable, a lady killer
By ladies killed or lit,
A bulb on a string,
Me being the string puller.
I lay on him desire
Kiddish as an all-day sucker.
His act for me
Is that I be always
Ready,
Ready-or-not never,
Waiting just,
Willing just,
Still as jello in an unjoggled bowl
Until he dips the spoon.
I act his act for me and more,
Smiling at his soft obstinacy
My act of mercy.

IT COMES TO THIS

You swatted, knocked it off,
yet severed only the tail.
So it rose up and attached
itself to you again and burrowed in.
You dug it out with your nails.
We lived with it until its death
seemed normal. After a time
(simply, it was there so long)
it seemed like love.
It comes to this:
If I were to cross an unknown stream
you would tie a rope around,
my waist, one end to your own
or to a tree, if there is one.

SECOND LOVE

(March 22)

Last year this date it snowed,
Wind blew the cold to zero.
Not a bud unbuttoned, ground muffled,
Securing what was bound
For May's marshalling.

Today might lure the summer birds home.
Forsythia, crocus, jonquil
Push past the strictures of their history.
The sun is sirening. The cherry blossom
Has gone out on a limb.

IF I WERE THE STONE

If I were the stone you stumbled on,
you would see, beyond your bruises,
an object blameless in your path.

The hunter's sure forgiveness
is the dying deer's unkowningness.

If we could, by some miraculous excision
from our selves, forgive, we would be,
would we want it? The stone. The deer.

CHAIR

Here it stands
as Luther would have
his Articles stand—
an incontrovertible
conclusion.
Let a child clamber
on its singular upholstery
with gloves of jam;
let pornographers
perform in its lap;
shroud it a hundred years
and it will wait
to be unshrouded
until time deposits new warm
bodies and appraising eyes.
Let a madman rage it to splinters,
it will coruscate in infinity,
dancing toward zero
like any other star,
utterly obedient,
utterly passive.

FLOOR MEDITATION

Nothing, no skin of water
Without mosquito wake
On most windless of days
So quiet as untrodden floors,
So patient as girders in dusky basements,
Bearing the whole house over them
Except in their seasonless dockage
The dead.

DANDELION MORAL

Tough old woman of a harsh land,
practice well your tricks; elevate,
as though it were not you, body
of a slim girl, supple as wind.
Stand her en pointe to balance her
being's gold, to die her own death,
release her own ashes to wind.
Give up your name to her, while you
crouch among grasses digging wells.

HELEN'S DREAM

I was scrawny as a mouse,
my hair like chicken down.
I lunged. I thought my heart
would burst, beat the shell
with my skull. A shard
just missed my throat.
My sister just lay there
not caring if she was born.
She knew.

IF

If time be upon you like a plug,
Do not, therefore, test the hone of knives
With the edge of your thumb, nor count
The floors from balcony to pavement,
Nor envy your neighbors their gas ovens.
For though your self succumb, yet your other
Self will bend over you and breathe
Into your mouth

HOOK

You cut the worm in half

To bait a hook for God,

But heads and tails

Grow heads and tails.

EZRA'S MOTHER

She looks nineteen
though she is twenty-seven, and plays
the guitar, between wide open thighs,
slung in a flowered dress like a cradle,
bent into the song with bony bare
shoulders and high tight breasts.
Even at breakfast
her eyes are full of tongues
that make old buddha-bellied boys
suck in. They follow her around.
So do the young.
Little son, little tinkler toy
Ezra, watch out,
your mama, oh what big teeth she has!

THE ONE SON

Sisters,
I was sixteen before I knew
The demarcations of our kitchen table,
The bruised and polished fruit,
The cake and day-old loaves.
My knickerbockers jangled
While you palmed your carfare,
Darned your hose.
Your mother was closed,
Mine, openhanded.
Yet, me being boy and baby,
You forgave me.

IMMIGRANT CHILD

My hair was scissored
straight across above the eyebrow,
straight across below the earlobe.
My dresses straight as paper dolls'
cut without pattern, front to back,
printed with flowers that laundered out
like snowflakes in April.
I carried lunch in the *Freiheit*
Pa read the night before,
leaning on the porcelain kitchen table.
My spectacles were tiny portholes
framed in steel, from the Department
of Relief. "Not prume, prune,"
said Mrs. Greg, the English teacher.
"Not gimp, limp." She flowed
in beige silk from desk to blackboard;
she stood before us in silk stockings.
Her lorgnette hung from a golden chain
to just the place the hand goes
when pledging allegiance to the flag
of the United States of America.

LILA

His touch woke me.
God, the night was hot.
The room smelled, somehow,
of my father, his bedroom,
his underwear.
Smelled of the perfume
the man bought me, fit
for his blue-eyed princess, he said,
in its beautiful midnight velvet box
with real five-pointed stars,
not these pinholes in the sky.
Turning my face in the pillow,
pretending to sleep, I opened my thighs,
moved slightly against his hand.
I knew when he soaked his pajamas.

WAR STORY

Mother wore him on her arm
As an amulet. He was the jewel
She wore at her throat
He was her fur-trimmed coat
She hung him as a blue star
In the living room window, over the mohair sofa
Facing the street. On February 25, 1943
She hung him as a gold star.

CODE

Bone Blood Tongue Lobes Thumb
Chromosome-coded:
Am I not smart? Am I not pretty? Am I not quick?
How dumb I am! How ugly! Tricked with sin!
Countersigning adjectives around a noun
Until the code breaks down
Rebound
In clumps of flower
Lumps of clay.

ZYGOTE

Icarus
in a dark cocoon
spinning his wings
winging his doom

TO A LOVER

The garlands and laurels

set on the foreheads

of those who fought best

sang best

on you

should be placed

lower

no

lower.

YOU ARE

To say this, he knelt
on the ground, his lips so close
her petals moved upon his breath,
"Dear Violet," he said with all his heart,
"You are my most beloved flower."
The next day, with all his heart
He said, "You are" to the rose.

LEAVING

I looked into your eyes
and found you ugly

and found you beautiful as rain

I pulled my breast from your mouth
and turned my back on you

and loved you with my back

SYMBOLS AND SIGNS

Birds carpet the sky, too close
to see the pattern of their flight

which rips sharply, falls
rustling ragged edges among oak leaves

and the tree bends and creaks as though
its greenness camouflaged rings of decay.

Each bird would scarcely tip a leaf.
Each note would tap the air

the way a droplet tunes an April pool:
The way to know the Furies

is that they do not come singly.

SOMEONE'S SONS

A boy galloped toward me, a big, gangling
boy, too old to gallop. Arms carried out front,
dangling hands, and head out front, like a horse
sniffing wind, but not like a horse—heavy-footed,
splayed, as though the one thing learned
was that the ground might move before the feet
returned.

His companion, younger by a span, kept
doubling back, not to gain on him too far.
His head carried the sky, the way they teach
posture school. I knew he would toss me
a glittering "Hi!" And that the other,
loose-lipped, uttering a thread of spittle,
would level me to stone, to tree, impartial
as geometry.

ROOMS

A room with no windows
is the universe:
Lay-Z-Boy, reruns
flickering on a screen.
Wall mirrors tighten it.
A room with no windows
disappears into its mirrors.

A room with windows is dangerous—
its tributaries widen in airy tangles
impossible to trace or bring
to just conclusion. Though elegantly
furnished, galaxies admonish it,
though tenanted and titled
unleased.

FACING THE MAGDALENS

Out here the water is like liquid land
and the wind out of the north never dies,
and I am not myself. The seaside woods
seems a city throng held in a green spell
by the wand of the thirteenth godmother—
the one who undoes the evil—
held so long passive and peaceful that if
it were kissed into dance, the dance would be
of passivity and peace. I know how
the forest feels from my childhood's game
of statues, when I would whirl and whirl
out of myself, out of my child worry
and child solitude and freeze a while
in a happy enthrallment of angel
or gargoyle or princess or buffoon.

HI-RISE HAIKU

1.
So loud, my footsteps
on the packed snow

    cicadas sleep undisturbed

2.
while eating an apple
I watch
the ripe moon in my window
hang secure

3.
on the tenth floor
neither rain nor snow

    a bird looks me in the eye

4.
your image in the high window
lights candles, sips wine

alone in the garden
I look up

5.
when owls lie wisely down
dogs down the street
awake crowing

6.
fireplace ashes
still this morning shaped like logs

all-night a wet snow
has covered everything

7.
my walls white as gunpowder

somewhere a hare hides in fields of snow

8.
in a winter wood
one gathers
another kindles

in my crystal vase
one gardenia glows

9.
empty Smirnoff
stands full of evening

footsteps of strangers
fill with snow

10.
O seagulls
you must be demented—
far from the living water

11.
Three hundred mail slots and no word from you

The petals of all flowers fall silently

12.
Overhead, fifteen ceilings
Underfoot fifteen floors
Neighbors, do you hear my dancing?

LATE LOVE

I sit in the audience watching
my hands get older while the poet reads
from "Elegies for the Living." *Nothing
dies forever*, he assures us, *yet
comes a time so much of life is gone,
new love is good as gone already . . .*
And I am thinking about how I saw
someone like you, new love, on TV,
on top the Chestnut filly who placed
in the Belmont. Her legs were swift as whips.
You leaned hard along her neck, kissed her ear,
goaded her toward trophy and wreath
. . . but be consoled, the poet says, *Late love
can not be lost for as long a time
as old love.*

THE LIE

When I tell you I love you
it is a lie

When I tell you I do not love
that too is a lie

Do you believe either?

Which? And why?

And if I stay with you
day by year

Whispering one of them
in your ear

Until the day I die

Would you believe the lie?

ROACHES

Put yourself in their skins.
Look closely at this one
transfixed on your counter top
like a deer in headlights—
antennae a millimeter longer
than the common lot, the flirtatious way
it now prances from cupboard
to wall, the markings on its anterior wing
like a candle flame, its toes
delicate as seedlings. One could
fall in love with long looking.

43

THEREFORE

If a dog attack you the wound will heal
though there remains a ragged scar.
But if your heart attack you
the wound will not heal,
for the heart is a rabid dog.
Therefore,
do not pace, plotting and planning
amongst the mighty on the hilltop,
but in the valley run
with those that chance the stray bullet,
for the aim of many is poor,
and the space between bullets
is silent and peaceful.

MR. MANN

Among the cattle on the plains of slaughter,
Mr. Mann's derricks keep bowing
to the Lord of More.

Mr. Mann's dog has been let out
of the bronco limousine to run on the mountains.
He chases rabbit and obeys the Lord of Turd.

And driving on the highways
between his ranches, past brown cows
and white cows, long horns and short horns,
and speckled calves still weak in the knees
Mr. Mann speaks:
Yum, he says, yum, yum.

OUR GIFT

Make small cuts in male viaducts,
nips and tucks in oviducts
and it is over.
Little pain, little blood.
Everything done for estate will stop.
Everything done for monument will stop.
All reasons but the reasons of grass
will stop.
After a brief yesterday, all
will be mosses, feathers, claws, clouds.
Rain will be rain, wind, wind.
Absented of us
all will be a holy rolling,
a whirling, a quaking.
After our compassionate abandonment
trackless as a flight of birds.

PUZZLE

So many,
the sky is pieces of blue jigsaw
between them.   So many,
the snow geese
are one thing—like a blizzard
that knows its destination
                    And all survive,
except for the wing-impaired,
or the laggard, caught in the hem of
a whirlwind.
            And who would notice
one imperfect departure—
one fall?
            God, how much life there is!
Beetles and blades of grass—
each one different as fingertips.
            Yet no fingertips
except where there is grass,
no grass except where there are beetles.
                    All one piece.
The snow geese's inexorable flight.
The snow goose's fall.

THE VIGIL

Neitzsche saw it, and prayed for it to molt,
not shadowy, in history, but traced
in every common Weimar face, as he
sat sickening at his sister's side.
Jeffers saw wings whipping air and eyes sharp
as spurs. Melville, squat on his low stool, saw
a finger motionless and blank between
the digits on the page, and blank the scrolls
rolling on New Bedford's sea.
                    So be it!
cried Neitzsche, *I will improve upon it*
then. Create it longer, blacker, thicker.
Melville consoled himself with absolute
despair. Jeffers saw an eagle eat it
in whose gut it lives and breeds. And I
hunger for any digestible lie.

MIDNIGHT SNOW

White rune on obsidian

What it says will be said over and over

Before it is understood

You can take your time

PART II   THE TRADE

THE TRADE

1.

You had your pick
of the hothouse rosebed of a Vassarclass,
you, Viking-bearded poet,
young enough to afford, than they, to be much older.

Old enough to know by their flushing,
their eyeing of the floor, which slim
dormitory bed had dreamt you the night before,
wanting to be loved as only a poet could love,
wanting to be the one rose pressed
between collected poems.

Of these you plucked
a lovely fatherless idolater,
who flashed at you
sparrow's wristbones
from under cashmere sweaters
and gestures, between arm and arm,
of a kitten playing with two small balls of yarn.

Poetry was your calling card and royal seal,
your other lady, safely mermaid-bottomed.
You had your pick,
thought you could have them both.
You didn't note the slight already shrivel of the stone,
webbing of your own limbs.

Rosebud was your twelve years wife
while what commanded centuries of eloquence
diminished to the size of home.

2.

Suppose someone were king of the mountain,
commanding horses and legions of men,
and had three daughters
named Goneril, Cordelia, and Regan.
Would someone write about them?
reclused in a lonely room
with the door closed
and curtains pulled against the moon?

No. He would sit his girls on his lap,
his little moppets,
smelling of licorice and cherry candy,
and they would twirl the hairs on his beard
with their little handies,
and pass happily his life that way
chucking their tiny fat chins.

But suppose someones come and plop
them atop stallions
and whisk them away like the wind,
and him so enraged he names them again,
Gonorrhea, Cornmelia, and Raccoon,
and stomps the ground and pisses at the moon.

Now he has the time and the misery and the topic.

3.

No coin is lost, the change
merely shifted from pocket to pocket.

4.

Now he wrote.
He wrote sheets; he wrote sheaves;
he wrote the moon in letters;
he wrote wristbones and licorice and stallions.
And he adjusted his mind to his mirror
and wrote epilogues and postscripts and old men writing,
and wrote Rosebud
forty years ago,
her delicate shoulders inclined above the book,
one fine strand of pale hair
falling across the deep well of voice
as she read the end of Lear,
loved as only a poet could love—
Look there. Look, there!

SUBJECT MATTER

Real life goes on
outside these fragments,
marches
to land's end.
These fragments,
like little kids, Little Leaguers
in uniforms inscribed Poetry Lives
try to catch some moments
and throw them back into the playing field.

There was a poem
I reached for years ago:
cannibalism in the Andes—
an airplane crash, a mountain blizzard.
I knew that after the man was saved
and returned to wife and son
he would forsake them, and that the poem
would have a kind of hyena humor, the son
would ask, Dad, where's Joe, and dad would say,
I ate him, and then he would leave.
I knew it would end years later in the tropics
with distention--the man's blue-veined stomach
throbbing, another's hand stroking it,
and the man saying, feel. He still moves.

But I knew no more.
Or if I knew
I could not say.

. . . the quick brown fox jumps over the fence
the quick brown fox jumps over the barbed wire fence

the red-brown fox with the wet black nose like a friendly
dog jumps over the broken electric barbed wire fence
the fox the color of harvests or sunsets or
bloody vomit jumps over the metal reach of the law,
rushes onto the pretty chickens causing breakfast
and terror and knowledge.

REVISIONS

8/8/83 first draft

New friend,
we come
to each other
like the Tarot
Man With a Pack On His Back

What it contains
is a mystery
the cards will unfold
if we read correctly
as they turn in time

But the pack is there
and cannot
be ignored
and will cast
on the future like bones
like light and shadow

Will old heart wounds
leak onto our arms?
Will we put mail on
our new linked arms?
Will old loves rise
and not let us close?

Must we carry the pack,
self-conscious and ashamed

of our lumbering gait,
into this new wide and unsullied meadow?

9/2/83 second draft

New love,
we come to each other
like the Tarot
Man with the Pack, the Fool,

who stretches
at the edge of a cliff
to catch a butterfly,
one foot already thrusting into space,
the grounded foot
nipped by a snarling dog.

From here
I see only the top
of the edge, which may be
the ragged shoulder
of a shallow trough,
or the rim of a nonperilous
drop. If below is a chasm,

will The Fool be broken on rocks?
or will his pack catch on something,
transforming all into a comedy of errors?
or will the butterfly
grow powerful as Pegasus?
The lunge forward

already has
precipitated the end.

We'll see.

10/22/83 third draft

    Love,
we came to each other
like Tarot's Fool,
on the axis of a triangle,
hauling a pack of paraphernalia.
The next card,
the one that isn't shown,
unfolds The Fool
doing a jig and laughing,
bells on his fool's cap chiming
merrily in an open meadow
which may be space or time or love,
suspended

11/12/83

Love, let him go,
the joker who came with the cards.
Who cares
if he is dangling in space still

or crashed on the rocks. We are
here in bed,
holding each other.

THE VERY IRIS

A spring flower before its season,
an iris—fringed mauve
lightening to lavender,
deepening to purple
around a golden lip:

I see a tiger tongue about to swallow
I see golden caterpillars
crawling toward their hibernation
and the feathery, deep-veined amethyst
they will become

I see the hidden timpani
of an enchanted ear

a deep-set Oedipal eye:

myself in all the guises of metaphor.

Only the eye repeats the almost flower
only at the infinitesimal point of gaze
which later, more and more,
becomes a measure of itself,
and then an iris poem.
Only the iris
translates itself in iris skin.

Even so,
if I were a painter
I would be a Realist,
attempt the very iris—

the waxy-white-powdered-with-mother-of-pearl-
each-yellow-hair-minutely-separate-
along-nameless-continuums-of-something-we-call-purple
iris, the sheer impossibility of it
a tribute.

How fortunate for poets
words
don't grow in fields.

THE WRONG SIDE OF THE BED

You can meander.
You see a violet from the path
you saunter in for a close up
then a streak of wing and a call from above
and you're off

peering up between leaves
beyond trees

until bullfrog's grunting
urges toward water
and whatever surprises
of lily pad or pebble
the path unfolds

and before you know it
you have meandered a long and various way

while I stay
a stone's throw from the roadway
grooming aphids off the underside
of a violet.

And if next week, next month
I plan a farther excursion
I pause at the violet
unable to go on
without looking
and of course I find
the aphids back again.
Damn!

When you return
emblazoned with yarns
I sit dumb and envious and listen,
my story being always the same story
about the many aphids
and the one violet

and how it spreads its petals humbly on its stem
and how its colors move
over the surface of its petals
in many shades and hues of mauve
and purple, for which I have no names.

JUST WATCHING

Imagine a bird flying a flower
up to decorate its nest. Or Giraffes
ignoring laden fig trees to gawk
at a sunset. Imagine a whole tribe
of chimpanzees on a Saturday night,
wheeling their old, hoisting their children,
and thronging in feathers and shiny shoes,
halooing and touching hands along the way,
to a dedicated spot where they all
will sit very still, doing nothing, just
sitting, like the surrounding trees and the rocks
they sit on and the convexed air, watching
one of them whistle. That we can may save us.

POETRY IN THE PARK

Words tossed up
like juggling
golden balls on a summer day
gather crowds, kids

gleeful and awful,
gather light,
then drop
into the dark pit of the throat

then skyward again

with aplomb! the fountaining,
the plain audacity of it!

outwrought—
the apposable thumb of speech,
most flexible of languages,
shaping love and death,
and the crowd listening, almost believing
until they are pulled away to
home, supper, bed—
similitudes.

HELEN - THE WORD

The word rings for attendants—
Hades, horses, hair, hurt, hubris, Hector,
exhilarations, hyperventilations—poems.
She lives as figment of imagination.
                                        Helen's heart,
startled animal,
utterly unrhetorical, wholly, by Helen even
(so seduced she was by words) unknown
and dead forever.
Helen who never was lives on
in mental aberrations,
apparitions—poems.
Oh the vanity
of these incrustations.

Hubris—the word recurs:
Helen—the aspiration of our language
to capture her
and Homer and heaven all in one breath.

Poetry fodder.

What's simply loved
can't be written.

Just plain 'elen.

THE PERFECT READER

The poets are making pictures
of their perfect reader (the one
who is not a listening god
or answering self but perfectly
other)

a seventh grader from the Sacred Heart,
hips still swathed in baby fat, and the book
held so close to myopic innocence
that all the world outside the book is vague
periphery

the one in the college bookstore
on a rainy night, who stands for an hour
to read the poems, then spends her $3.95
on a vinyl slicker

the one on the ten-speed racer,
the book left dog-eared and face down,
clouds of hair spinning behind her, "blissed out,"
as one poet said

the child full of sin who vows
on the wall behind the calendar
abstinence from that day forward,
then reads "Thanatopsis" or "Beautiful
Annabelle Lee," then reads them again,
out loud, with feeling

but I would like my poems to be
pinball machines with silver balls;

my perfect reader works the flippers
and gives just enough English to almost
make it tilt.

FORSYTHIAS

So brave in the unexpected snow,
yellow feather of the forward guard,
nearer promise for those who never quite
believe when winter comes it isn't here
to stay. Munificent, it blooms in February
if you bring it in, stays, by cutting back,
till May: yet modest, it squanders all its gold
then retires in humble green behind
the larkspur and the rose. A starry plant,
easy to sentimentalize. Grander
than this have been deceived by the eye
of the beholder. Knowing this I look
at it in a different way:

Not brave but braggadocio. (Snowflowers
have blossomed for a month, audacious
little tongues under footfalls of the ignorant.)
Odorless, it proves again to those
experience has taught there's no reward
for drawing near. Gluttonous, every limb
that touches ground becomes a root.
Egoist, it waves, "I'm here!" as though
it weren't duplicated up and down
the street at each garage: My bush. My speech.
My tendency to turn a golden
opportunity to black and white.

Yet yearly, still unspoken for, the one
out there makes effortless transformations,

pre-inscribed, while this one, by summer
unachieved, goes on revisioning,
struggling to flower before it leaves.

FOR PHILIP LARKIN

Frightening to one who lives
alone, the thought of the sudden trip
to emergency. Unexpected
death under the knife hardly worse
than imagining the unknown doctor
attempting to locate a cousin
or some friend, who, found,
would be dismayed to learn a week had passed,
during which, if one had been thought of
at all, had been pictured
in the satisfying boredom
of a bachelor's routed rounds,
a week since, gasping for air,
one may have talked into the line
that opens in The Nearest Hospital,
summoning rescue.
No children, never married,
an only child oneself, there's no one
for anyone to send condolence to.
But if one is poet laureate
of consternation, demographer
of the common woe, the world's eyes
are smudged with one's obituary,
and one's voice is left behind, difficult
to describe as the taste of tomato.

DAEDALUS TECHNOLOGIES, INC.

What flies this green morning
while the sun burns away
the mist? Uncle's glider planes,
the kids' kites, the airmail letter
from Icarus mother waits for
in the sun by the mailbox.
Nothing mythical.

What melts this heavy afternoon?
Ice cream cones down forearms,
bubble gum to root a foot—
nothing in peril,
except perhaps the inventory
of Daedalus Tech, Inc.
Chapter Eleven.
Nothing tragic.

What fell? My brother?
Or a NASA rocket.
Or a Goodyear blimp.
Or even Dad's newest invention—
a man-shaped helium balloon, which,
if ever found, would be only shriveled rubber.
No one ever mentions
the insurance policy,
the cool million.

TO BE A POET

Come from a harsh father, and a mother
of whims. Run from the blows of the one
and sometimes catch the other
in a milky mood. Run from the snarl and nip
of the other and sometimes catch the one
with a tender muscle. Thus do you learn
freezing and burning and how to be
a windcock in variable weather.

Light runs before you on the ground, parting
red tides of shadows. Do not lift your eyes
to find the source of the light. Do not watch
for signs at the crossroad. Bless the providence
that saved you from the couch, the bench, and the bed
and set you down to chase the light
on the running ground, the alpha and zed
from which the world was created.

OLDER THAN BEFORE

Having lifted to the cold-eyed mountain,
I care to write poems about the young—
not, as earlier, the mainstream young
who dream smiling of the rose of death

and rush into the arms of love and war,
or those rarer tragedians who strike
out in heroic anger at what's wrong.
I mean the very young—infant and toddler

and child 'till ten (by twelve already,
long noses and strings). I mean this little
crawling one, poking a virgin finger
into a meat grinder, into a mousetrap,

into a socket, or this one, the wind
itself, laughable, on feet so small
you could take the whole of one in your mouth,
toward the insouciant traffic, or this one

unhelmeted, accelerating, letting
go, lifting off. I care to write about,
that is, the ones who live by grace, the ones
who live guiltless of the watchful other.

FROM THE CREATIVE WRITING CLASS

"Write," said the teacher,
"a modest poem. No
earthshake, no
well of trauma
from some impossible past, no
fate of earth; write
a little thing, biodegradable,
a disposable wrapper,
write a glass of water or
eating a peach or buying 'em,
write soapsuds and shaving . . . "

"But," said the student the following week,
"as soon as I thought of shaving
I thought of my father,
leaning against the washbowl, face
lathered to the whitebeard
I'd never see, screwing his mouth up,
turkish towel slung around his neck,
slapping on a good scent
I craved to follow like spoor,
and whistling out the house
and the house settling back
into its prose. Every day the same
including the day the house stayed that way.
And when I thought of peaches
I thought of how they used to taste,
and the produce man at Super M explaining,
Ohio peaches are almost gone since winters
stay so long, cutting the season
to what only apples can ripen on, and I hear

my old aunt saying, Cleveland winters
never did till now grab autumn so far in
and knowing now why the tips of my little fingers
get numb earlier every year, and putting
the plastic bag and the peaches
picked green in California
back. And when I thought of a glass of water
I thought of the time it hadn't rained
for thirty days and how the birds in the birdbath
raised small clouds of dust
and the cracking of warblers' necks
on the shimmering windows . . .

MMMMM - MMMMM

The times when every poet

Is too sticky-sweet to swallow

When the best submerge and wallow

In a tub of toffee

There is a thing the stomach can endure

Carminative, the dill and brine

Of Marianne Moore.

NEVER PUT ICARUS IN A POEM ABOUT AIRPLANES

or Pegasus, either.
And never put Icarus
in a poem about candles or moths.

Though looking at this moth and this candle
you can't help thinking about Icarus.

You manage to get the moth out of the poem,
but not out of your head, where it circles
the candle as though flame and wing
were one object.

Meditate upon the candle—
leaf of light, rivulets of lava,
moth curled on the table—
a scrap of love note—
then
if Icarus re-enters
the foundry of your eyes
return him to the poem.

THINKING OF ANNE SEXTON

1.

I can hardly imagine you
wheeling a baby carriage
in the park, your mind
drifting idly with the leaves,
warm in a good wool coat,
now and then smiling
at nothing in particular,
merely being simple,
merely submissively being here.

2.

I read you first in Harpers in 1959,
dark webs to catch your husband
snoring in his blowzy bag.

Since then, footprints
of a whole sad clan, boozed-up
father, whose fly you unzipped in public,
mother, whose womb you fitted
to our monocle, daughter
whose head you shaved, led
slowly through the streets,
crying flesh and bone, alive, alive, oh.

3.

Your dust cover eyes
reveal the awful rowing.

But up on stage
your voice commanded us
like a foghorn in a sea of canoes,

urged us to the dark vortex
where your voice filled our lungs
and we understood what is dying.

We emerged to a dazzle of sunlight
surprised to find how beautiful
were the whores, the drunks, the stray dogs.

4.

There is always a corpus delicti
and prints of the guilty,
though they be gathered into a rag
or hidden in the sweaty darkness of a glove:
but with you we had only the corpus of the killer
and the print of the victim.

Cherchez la femme.

If you had murdered anybody else
you could have copped a plea.

5.

Are you happy now
my sad-eyed Anne?
Are you with the morning dove

at the top of the tree?
With the solitary hawk?

WHICH QUICK BROWN FOX?

When the quick brown fox jumps over the fence

is it a specific fox
that jumps this one time for this particular writer?

Or is it

THEFOX,

from The Kingdom-of-Fox,

as in, "The Fox is incapable of mercy"?

If it is this unique, never to be duplicated fox,
then the jump
over
needs further definition:
1) a dragged foot
and a thatch of fur on barbed wire,
2) an unfinished arc
with blood at its severed end
3) a perfect half moon
that rises from one side of the fence
and descends in the midst of chickens.

But if it is THEFOX,
then OVER is a transcending of fence.
THEFOX always lands where it wants.

But if it is this fox,
whose hungry young await its return,
then "over" is critical,
and "to jump over" an imperative of survival.

But if THEFOX,
"jumpover" is essentially a unitary
act, and "over" redundant.

The meaning of "over," then, is entirely dependent
upon the meaning of "fox," not to mention the meaning
of "fence" which may encircle a sqawkage of chickens
or may be more pure and luminous than the moon
the cow jumped over.

AND THAT'S THAT

In the year 2001 my first poetry book was published.
I was 60 years old.
In 2002 another book of poems was published.
In 2003 another book of poems was published.
I had been writing poems all my life.
Also in the year 2003 I inherited $1 million
(no fooling), when my stepfather, who hated me,
finally died. I had been poor all my life.
Not without shelter poor, or food poor, or movies poor,
but dining at the Friendly Inn sort of poor, winter jacket
from K-Mart sort of poor. In the year 2004 I died.

A WOMAN'S WILL

This is no pastime for a married woman.
The sail grabs your hand, billowing
like Queen Victoria's righteousness,
but whisks you swift and unbound down-

current. There the wind subsides. Becalmed,
the sail stutters like a fibrillating
heart, like a bedeviled weathercock,
and you are assailed by scents you built up high

to avoid: lymph and muckwart and acrid
ash of your own house burning on the hill.
Your husband, on the other hand, knows how
to utilize the most modest of winds,

to tease, tack from one shore to the other
zigzagging, never running aground,
and always slightly upwind of the odor.
Whom can you blame for this state of affairs?

Patriarchy's five thousand years?
Jesse Helms? The Pope? Might as well
blame the propositions of poets—

A boy's will is the wind's will.

EMILY DICKINSON AT HOME

Which way is North? I've not forgot
But periwinkle and middle age deride
The soul's Pretension that the world
Is Home

Sherry myopias, the span
Of hands on garden gate and walls
Measure all my universe, almost all
I've loved.

I was never one who,
twisted and turned in blindman's buff,
could then infallibly reach out and find
And hold.

Stationed in my quiet spot
I did require no eyes to tell
What ever so heavily hangs
Over head.

Sequestered now in a shrinking South
Under a heaven of self-named stars
I steer between marble and my tufts
Of poems.

FOR WALT WHITMAN

Poor Unrequited lover of the darkness,
Expecting warmth and softness of a mother-kiss
Enormous must have been your disappointment
Coming face to face with emptiness.

Arch Sensualist!
You rouged death's cheek
And curled his hair,
Perfumed him with lilac
And gave him lark's song
To make sweet calling noises,
And yourself seduced yourself.

STUDY POEM

If you would know the sea,
mix your orgasm with its waters.

If you would alter the apple,
eat it.

If you would recognize the world,
observe yourself.

If you would love the world,
remember yourself.

If you would love the world,
forget yourself.

If you would recognize the world,
look at the world.

If you would alter the apple,
change your idea of apple.

If you would know the sea,
keep dry.

Questions

1. The first half of the poem presents a series of aphoristic
statements that the poet expects you to accept as true. After
reflecting on each statement do you agree that it is true? **2.** The
second half of the poem, a mirror image of the first, also presents a
series of truisms. However, these are diametrically opposed to the

first four. Do you find the second series to be true? Do you find them in contradictory relationship with the first series? If you answer yes to both these questions, then you are dealing with antinomies, that is, two statements each of which is true yet each of which cannot be true if the other is true. The syllogism of an antinomy would be: If A=B and B=C, then C=F. Or perhaps it would be, if A=B and B=A, then A=C.

Suggestions for Writing

1. Using the two halves of the poem as models, try writing a third half which would be equally true. For example, "If you would know the sea,/make a union of H2O and NaCl. Perhaps that is not such a good example. Make up your own.

THE TRADE 2

The baby pigeon didn't survive
the springtime's sudden glut of snow,
and I cried, seeing the twin stiff legs
protrude from under the thaw,

and a voice said, easy tears?
What will these tears buy?
From where do these tears come?
from greater-love-than-this,
the storehouse of all good?
or perhaps the storehouse only
of right arms?
of eyes?
of fingernails?
Tell me, taunted the voice,
would you give the smallest nail
of your more awkward hand
to have the bird alive?

But if, my retort ran,
I gave all ten
I could save only ten
out of an infinite sky.
One fingernail?
I looked at the bird
and stood,
half expecting a flutter at my feet
and on my hand a softness
as under a new-pulled tooth.

Then I went inside
and thought how seldom
death will trade with us
and thought of the absurd
consolations we construct and call poems,
where, we insist, the dead
cast skipping stones, where the dead
still ripple,

knowing our insistence hogwash,
knowing poems are only, but are,
our eyewash.

ABOUT THE AUTHOR

Lolette Kuby was a life-long Clevelander until she decided to move to Canada five years ago. At the age of six (the year she learned to write), she wrote her first poem. Though the muse visited sporadically for many years, she didn't demand permanent entrance until Lolette was in grad school working on a doctorate in English at Case Western Reserve University. After receiving her Ph.D., Lolette taught at Cleveland State University for fourteen years.

Lolette's poems have appeared in scores of well-known literary journals and in a chapbook. Her first full-length collection was published in 2002. Poetry is her first, but not her only love. She writes in many genres— literary criticism, short fiction, & magazine articles. Her move to Canada took her out of the university classroom and into full-time freelance editing of poetry and fiction.

Also by Lolette Kuby
An Uncommon Poet for the Common Man: A
Study of Philip Larkin's Poetry (literary criticism)
In Enormous Water (Poetry)
The Mama Stories (Short Fiction)
Faith and the Placebo Effect: An Argument for
Self-healing (Non-fiction)
Set Down Here (Poetry)